God to the Heart of a Wife
© God to the Heart of a Wife, all rights reserved. No part of this publication may be distributed, transmitted, or reproduced in any form or by any means, including recording, photo copying, or other mechanical or electrical method, without prior written permission from the author. Scripture is taken from the Holy Bible. New International Version®, NIV®. Copyright© 1973, 1978, 1984, 2011 by Biblica, Inc.® Used by permission of Zondervan. All rights reserved worldwide.
ISBN – 978-1-7336 203-3-8

Dedication

 To my mother, Shirley Dewese the heart of a mother who has represented GOD well. Your example and touch of love in the lives of others will live on after you are gone. Your heart reflects the beauty of heaven. To Edna Ramirez whose life represents the simplicity of God's love this side of Heaven. You both have enriched my life, leaving my heart full of gratitude!

Preface

Things are continually changing as the immoral and loose standards of society swirl around us. It is important to remember who we serve and whose we are.

This book is all about God's heart and what he is saying to you as a wife. God loves you and your desire to love, honor, and respect your husband brings boundless joy to his heart. As you read through this book, try to visualize the heart of God speaking directly to you. It does not matter who you are, where you have been or what you have done. God sees you through the blood and he calls you a woman after his own heart.

I pray this book refreshes you, as you spend time with God in his presence embracing what his heart, is saying to you as a wife. God is calling women to fill their role with hearts embracing honor and respect for their husbands. He has placed a high value on you as a wife and your role is priceless to God. His heart is for your marriage and loving him while honoring your husband, is gold.

Heaven is watching and cheering you on!

let all that YOU DO BE done in love
IICOR 16:18

the prayer
OF A RIGHTEOUS PERSON
is powerful and effective.

JAMES 5:16

YOU ARE
A WOMAN AFTER MY OWN HEART

Father God,

I ask you to help me love my husband today through your heart. As you gently lay things on my heart, I will love him with your goodness. Give me understanding and wisdom. Help me daily to trust you completely. I love you Jesus!

Amen

> There is power in your prayers!

you can totally do this

A wife of noble character is her husband's crown, but a disgraceful wife is like decay in his bones.
Proverbs 12:4

As you spend time with God today, write down the things he shares with you as he shows you how to love your husband.

Use these lines to record God's faithfulness.

_____

_____

_____

_____

_____

_____

_____

_____

_____

_____

_____

_____

_____

_____

_____

_____

_____

_____

_____

_____

Above all else, guard your heart, for it is the wellspring of life. Proverbs 4:23

Tender moments to grow your love

Guard Your Thoughts

Be careful of the thoughts you think about your husband. If they are not positive or team building, throw those thoughts away. Your thoughts will affect your actions. Guard your mind and only invite good thoughts to stay! You will find every struggle, battle, or issue, starting with the way you think about the things that happen around you. As you throw negative thoughts away and exchange them for positive thoughts, you will find your feelings changing!

Remember you do not have to embrace every thought you think. You can be just as choosy over the thoughts you think, as you are the fruits and vegetables you buy in the store! If they are not good thoughts just throw them away!

Megan texted her husband Ryan and asked him if he could bring home some milk. She is preparing their supper and she needs milk to finish the mashing of the potatoes. Ryan walks in the door, and she runs to greet him and retrieve the milk. He forgets the milk and apologizes. Megan looks at Ryan with her eyes full of disappointment. She turns around without giving him a hug and she heads back to the kitchen upset and frustrated. Megan cannot believe he forgot the milk, why didn't he just say, "No, I can't pick up the milk."

Megan was given the opportunity to think the best about her husband and love him regardless of whether he had milk in his hand. Remember as you align your thoughts with heaven, your marriage, life, and relationships will change! God loves you and He enjoys the way you welcome Him into your love journey!

On the following lines, practice writing good thoughts about your husband. Make sure all your thoughts are good, positive, and uplifting!

My positive thoughts about my husband are,

_____
_____
_____
_____
_____
_____
_____
_____
_____
_____

My good thoughts help nurture my heart!

> *Feeding your marriage good thoughts are wise!*

God hovers over you with answers to the questions that lay upon your heart.

_____
_____
_____
_____
_____
_____
_____
_____
_____
_____
_____
_____
_____
_____
_____
_____
_____
_____
_____
_____
_____

Use these lines to record God's faithfulness.

_____
_____
_____
_____
_____
_____
_____
_____
_____
_____
_____
_____
_____
_____
_____
_____
_____
_____
_____

A gentle answer turns away wrath, but a harsh word stirs up anger. Proverbs 15:1

Tender moments to grow your love

Guard Your Words

Be careful of the words you speak about your husband and over him. There is power in your words. You will find yourself creating a world you live in with your words. Speaking good and positive things about your husband will make you wise. God enjoys your love words. No matter what happens or anything you find yourself faced with, choose to speak good things about your husband and others in your life!

Allison saw her husband Keith looking at pornography. She found her heart full of disappointment and hurt. She now has the opportunity, to tell her husband she is thankful for marrying a man who is faithful and has eyes for only her. She can also go to work; complain about him and say terrible things about her husband. **Which way do you think will produce good fruit?** Everything that happens to you will be an opportunity to produce good or bad. As you spread God's goodness in your relationships and marriage, you will experience His goodness surrounding you.

Allison decides to go to her prayer closet and pray for Keith. She thanks God for her husband and asks him to protect their marriage and to give her husband a heart of righteousness. She feels God's peace cover her heart. Allison then goes into the living room where he is sitting and gives him a hug. She tells him she missed him today. Allison sits down beside her husband and asks him about his day.

Do you think Allison's choice to love and pray for her husband Keith unconditionally helped grow her marital love? As a wife you will experience storms in your marriage, but when you choose to love and trust God it will be a total game changer! God's heart is for you, and he is with you through every marital disturbance.

On the lines below, speak good things about your husband! Remember to use only good words. If you think negatively, flip the switch, and speak positive things over the gift God has given you!

My husband is amazing at

_____
_____
_____
_____
_____
_____
_____
_____
_____
_____
_____

I enjoy the following traits about my husband,

_____
_____
_____
_____
_____
_____
_____
_____
_____
_____
_____
_____

My husband is a gift from God. I am grateful for the gift God has given me!

There is power in the words you speak!

your words will
BLESS OTHERS
as you
SPEAK
life over
PEOPLE AND
situations

Inhale God's presence today as you feel him hovering over you. He has all the answers you need!

Use these lines to record God's faithfulness.

_____
_____
_____
_____
_____
_____
_____
_____
_____
_____
_____
_____
_____
_____
_____
_____
_____
_____

My dear brothers, take note of this: Everyone should be quick to listen, slow to speak and slow to become angry, James 1:19

Tender moments to grow your love

Listen Well

Listen to your husband with the intent to understand him. Be careful not to listen just to answer him. This is a priceless tool that will grow your love. You will find your understanding growing as you focus on listening to the heart of your husband. The skill of listening will grow your love and nurture your relationship.

Eric came home from work and began to talk to Maggie about the things that had happened on his job site. She found herself bored with the conversation and began to think about some other things. She participated in the conversation with occasional wow's and oh my comments, without even hearing a word Eric was saying.

That next day Eric asked Maggie, "What do you think I should do?" She responded with, "About what?" Eric walked away with his heart sad. His loving wife had not heard anything he had said.

Do you think Maggie's actions nurtured their relationship? Remember to seize every opportunity to listen to the heart of your husband. When you listen to his heart you will develop a deeper understanding of him. God listens to you, and He longs for you to listen to your husband! Fill out the lines below and grow your marital love into a deeper place.

As I utilize the gift of listening, I have learned these things about my husband.

_____

_____

_____

_____

_____

_____

I understand to a greater level why my husband feels this way about...

_____
_____
_____
_____
_____
_____
_____

My husband is a gift from God and learning to understand him is a JOY!

> *Your love will grow with the art of listening!*

YOUR ABILITY TO HEAR MY VOICE WILL INCREASE YOUR ABILITY TO HEAR YOUR SPOUSE

As you spend time with God today, write down the things he shares with you as he shows you how to love your husband.

Use these lines to record God's faithfulness.

_____

_____

_____

_____

_____

_____

_____

_____

_____

_____

_____

_____

_____

_____

_____

_____

_____

_____

Therefore, as God's chosen people, holy and dearly loved, clothe yourselves with compassion, kindness, humility, gentleness, and patience. Colossians 3:12

Tender moments to grow your love

Be Thoughtful

Thinking about your husband when you are apart will grow your love. A simple love text at lunch or a phone call when you get off work, will remind him he is forever in your heart! Loving each other through communication is a marital necessity. You will find the characteristic of being thoughtful growing your love. As you continue to consider your husband's feelings, you will find your thoughtfulness maturing your relationship.

Carla had a dinner luncheon with her friends from work. She ordered the crab dinner and a second order to go for her husband Henry. She chatted with her friends for a few minutes, finished her food and took her to go order when she left.

When she got home, she found Henry watching the news. She went over to him, kissed his forehead, and reminded him how much she had missed him. Henry smiled and asked her, "Did you have an enjoyable time?" She responded by saying, "It would have been better, if I hadn't been missing you so much." He told her about his night and the two of them went to bed.

Henry got up the next morning and grabbed the lunch, Carla had made for him. He never knew what she had fixed but somehow, she always knew what he liked and wanted. That day at lunch when he opened his lunch bag, he found a nicely prepared crab dinner with a love note that said, "I missed you tonight, more than you know!" Henry smiled, as he read the note and began to think about his amazing wife! He pulled out his phone to call his one and only, to thank her for the thoughtful lunch!

Do you think Carla's thoughtfulness nurtured Henry's heart and grew their love?

Carla had the opportunity to forget about her husband and engage with her friends thinking only about herself and the moment in front of her. Instead, this amazing wife seized the opportunity to love her husband through the act of thoughtfulness.

As a wife, you will find yourself blessed with many opportunities daily, to love your husband. As you grasp all these moments, you will find yourself wise beyond your years! Today take the time to think about thoughtful acts you can do for your husband! To practice being thoughtful, fill out the lines below.

My husband's favorite food is,

_____

_____

_____

_____

My husband's favorite color is,

_____

_____

My husband's favorite sport is,

_____
_____
_____
_____

My husband's favorite restaurant is,

_____
_____
_____
_____

I can be thoughtful by,

_____
_____
_____

_____
_____
_____
_____
_____
_____

My husband is a gift from God. I treasure this gift by being thoughtful.

> *Your thoughtfulness is stunning!*

I LOVE YOU

with an everlasting love

Enjoy God's goodness today, as he shows you how your husband needs to be loved today.

Use these lines to record God's faithfulness.

For in the same way you judge others, you will be judged, and with the measure you use, it will be measured to you. Matthew 7:2

Tender moments to grow your love

Do Not Judge

Throw away judgment and be careful of finger pointing. Focus on the positives and choose to love. Just flip the switch and instead of noticing the bad or blaming your husband, focus on the good. Remember he is a precious, priceless gift from God! Be careful not to judge others. Once the door of judgment is open, you will find it easy to find fault with your husband and others in your life! Keep this door shut as you love and forgive each other daily!

Marcy found it easy to find fault with her husband Mick. When he tried to explain what had happened at work, she found it easy to blame him for getting laid-off even when it was not his fault. Mick packed his bags one day and told her he was done. He could not stay married to a woman who did not have his back. Marcy started crying and asked him to stay. She walked over to Mick and hugged him. She told him she was not aware that her actions were hurting him.

    The two of them sat down that night and talked to each other. Mick began to tell Marcy, about the things that had bothered him and why he needed her to stop. His mother had never trusted him and had always thought the worst about him. When Marcy second-guessed his actions, she was acting just like his mom. Marcy then told Mick she had watched her mom always doubt her dad. Her mom had never trusted her father on anything. Her parents later divorced but her actions were learned behavior from watching her parents.

    This amazing couple hugged each other as they shared stories and held hands. They prayed together, asking God to help them love each other better! Talking things out and loving each other is best no matter what the circumstance is.

    Do you think Marcy's ability to apologize for her wrong behavior helped Mick open up to her? Her effectiveness in listening to her husband had a huge impact on him. As a wife, you will receive multiple opportunities to nurture your marital love. It is important to embrace these moments and grow your love! Fill out the following lines and grow your marital love into a deeper place!

When I feel myself starting to be judgmental, I will,

_____
_____
_____
_____
_____

I will flip the switch and think positively by

_____
_____
_____
_____
_____
_____
_____

_____
_____
_____
_____
_____

My husband is a priceless gift from God. I appreciate and honor him by refraining from judgment!

YOU ARE
A CARRIER OF MY HOPE

Inhale God's presence today as you feel him hovering over you. He has all the answers you need!

Use these lines to record God's faithfulness.

_____
_____
_____
_____
_____
_____
_____
_____
_____
_____
_____
_____
_____
_____
_____
_____
_____
_____
_____
_____

He has made everything beautiful in its time. He has also set eternity in the hearts of men; yet they can not fathom what God has done from beginning to end.
Ecclesiastes 3:11

Tender moments to grow your love

Value Time

Value every moment together, the good and the bad. Time moves and cannot be stopped and once the moment is gone, you cannot get it back! Learn from the bad, increase the good and value your time together as precious and priceless! This will make you wise! Remember not to take anything for granted! Your love skills are amazing!

Mindy loved spending time with her husband. When her friends would ask her to join them, she would refuse if she knew her husband Jake was home. The two of them had been married 17 years. If you were to meet them, you would have thought they were newlyweds. They never got enough time together, and their date nights were the talk of their conversations with others.

Jake got sick and needed to see a doctor. He had been tired for a while but, started feeling extra drained. Dr Grant ran some tests and blood work. When the tests came back, Dr. Grant informed them both, he had 6 months to a year to live. They were both shocked. "What?" they said, at the same time. They left Dr. Grant's office holding hands but hanging onto hope. When they got to their car, Jake looked at Mindy and said, "My love, you have given me a life of love, and have shown me how to love." The two sat in their car just holding hands. **They both realized they had valued every moment and every opportunity to love each other**.

As they both went to bed that night; they found themselves grateful for valuing time. Do you think Mindy's capacity to value time, helped grow their marital love? Just like this incredible wife, you can value every moment with your husband no matter what happens.

Today take the time to reminisce over your life. Ask yourself, "Do I really value my husband and the time God has given us together?" Make sure, you can say "Yes," before it is too late! As you continue to value time, you will find yourself grateful for every moment.

As I value time, I find my heart grateful for,

_____
_____
_____
_____
_____
_____
_____
_____
_____
_____
_____
_____
_____

_____

_____

_____

_____

_____

My value for time prevents me from taking anything for granted.

> *Life is short.
> Treasure every moment
> as if it were your last!*

I MAKE ALL
things beautiful

God hovers over you with answers to the questions that lay upon your heart.

Use these lines to record God's faithfulness.

But just as you excel in everything, in faith, in speech, in knowledge, in complete earnestness and in your love for us, see that you also excel in this grace of giving.
II Corinthians 8:7

Tender moments to grow your love

Be Excellent

Excel at being a wife. You can just be married, have a marriage certificate, or excel at being the best. When you live above average and mediocrity, your excellence will make a difference in the lives around you! Excellence is your birthright! Utilize this right well! **Heaven is watching and cheering for you!**

Bruce and Yolanda had just gotten married. They had both been married before and they took their vows and commitments to each other seriously. Yolanda loved being a wife, and she looked after Bruce with care and excellence. Bruce was an attorney, who worked for a major firm. On his court days, he always needed to look his best. Yolanda faithfully ironed his shirts and pressed his pants the day before. He never had to ask her if she had washed his clothes. Yolanda would have his clothes pressed and laid out for the following day. Bruce loved this about His wife, and he always took the time to thank her with his words, kisses, and occasional flowers! Bruce knew he could invite his friends over at the last minute and their house would always be inspection ready.

Do you think Yolanda's excellence as a wife made an impact on her marriage? You will find your actions as a wife affecting your husband and the way he responds to you. This remarkable wife not only made her shine, but Bruce as well. Her care for her husband's schedule, and the things he needed, nurtured their love and marriage.

Today take the time to think about the things you do for your household and how you can improve on being more excellent.

I can be more excellent at,

_____

_____

_____

_____

_____

_____

_____

_____

To be excellent, I will ...

_____

_____

_____

_____

_____

Excelling in life at being an outstanding wife will grow my love!

Your excellence will grow your love!

I WILL
GIVE YOU UNDERSTANDING
AND YOU WILL SEE
THINGS THROUGH MY EYES

Inhale God's presence today as you feel him hovering over you. He has all the answers you need!

Use these lines to record God's faithfulness.

_____
_____
_____
_____
_____
_____
_____
_____
_____
_____
_____
_____
_____
_____
_____
_____
_____
_____
_____
_____

Words from a wise man's mouth are gracious, but a fool is consumed by his own lips. Ecclesiastes 10:12

Tender moments to grow your love

Use Love Phrases

Find love phrases or words you can give your husband to express your love. Your verbal expression of love is just as important as your actions. Your love words will nurture your relationship and grow your love. God enjoys the way you love your husband!

Melissa always had a way of expressing her happy feelings to Mark! She would thank him for marrying her and remind him, he was precious and priceless! Although words of affirmation, was not his love language, Melissa was feeding Mark's spirit good words of appreciation. Her gratitude to Mark for all he did for her was expressed through her actions and words. Their marital love grew and others around them admired the way they expressed their love to each other.

Do you think Melissa's gratitude, influenced their marital relationship? She was given opportunities to complain and nag Mark about things he should or should not be doing. Melissa chose to focus on the good and keep her heart full of gratitude.

Your role as a wife is important to God and He will always guide you and help you be the Godly wife your husband needs! Even though words of affirmation may not be his love language, when you speak you are feeding his spirit. Find good words you can feed his spirit.

My love phrases for my husband are

_____
_____
_____
_____

_____
_____
_____
_____
_____
_____
_____
_____
_____

My husband is a priceless gift from God I will treasure and value!

YOU ARE
A WOMAN WHO REPRESENTS ME WELL

As you spend time with God today, write down the things he shares with you as he shows you how to love your husband.

Use these lines to record God's faithfulness.

_____
_____
_____
_____
_____
_____
_____
_____
_____
_____
_____
_____
_____
_____
_____
_____
_____
_____
_____
_____
_____
_____

Drink water from your own cistern, running water from your own well. Proverbs 5:15

Tender moments to grow your love

Notice Your Husband

Use your eyes to notice your husband. Be ready to pick him up with God words when he is having an off day. Your faithful loving support through his hard days will nurture your relationship. God is faithful in noticing you and He loves the way you notice your husband.

Nicole worked the opposite hours of her husband, but she was always able to get home before he left for work. Tuesday, she found him sitting at the table looking down at the floor. He was not acting himself. Nicole walked into the room and said, "Baby, are you okay?" Nick looked up at her and said, "I am, now that you are here." He had just gotten a phone call from his brother, telling him their mother had been hit in a car accident. She had not made it. Tears filled Nick's face as he spoke. Nicole hugged Nick and reminded him that she was here for him. The two sat side by side on the couch as they shared stories they had together with Nick's mother. Nicole reminded Nick how much his mother loved him and how proud she was of him.

    Do you think Nicole's love and support helped nurture their marital relationship? This amazing wife loved Nick through the hard moments and was by his side through the funeral and the days to come. Their love grew with their honor and respect for one another!

    Today look for ways you can notice your husband and be ready to encourage, uplift and complement him. Remember he is a gift from God and your encouraging words bring immense joy to the heart of God! As you practice noticing your husband, you will find your love growing!

Today I noticed my husband

_____
_____
_____
_____
_____
_____
_____

The things I noticed about him, I never knew before were,

_____
_____
_____
_____
_____
_____
_____
_____
_____

My husband is a precious gift from God, I will notice and be grateful for daily!

I ENJOY THE WAY YOU LOVE YOUR HUSBAND! IT BRINGS GREAT JOY TO MY

HEART!

God hovers over you with answers to the questions that lay upon your heart.

Use these lines to record God's faithfulness.

_____
_____
_____
_____
_____
_____
_____
_____
_____
_____
_____
_____
_____
_____
_____
_____
_____
_____
_____
_____
_____
_____

Give thanks in all circumstances, for this is God's will for you in Christ Jesus. I Thessalonians 5:18

Tender moments to grow your love

Be Thankful

Always carry a heart of thanksgiving. Cultivating a heart of gratitude will nurture your love. When you could complain, just be thankful. You will find your love growing with your thanksgiving. Stay grateful and keep growing your love!

Wanda always had a way of expressing her gratitude to Justin no matter what was happening around her. If the glass was half empty, she found it half full. If she bought a twelve pack of pop and one can was empty, she was grateful for the 11 cans that were full. Justin was grateful for Wanda, and He thanked her for always being positive no matter what was happening around them! If Justin were having a difficult day, he would always express the events to Wanda in a negative way. She would listen to his day and express back to Justin, all the things he should be thankful for. He loved this about her and always found his heart grateful for her positivity.

Do you think Wanda's ability to see the good, helped nurture their marriage? This superb wife aided the growth of their love with her gratitude. She utilized every opportunity to express her appreciation for even the smallest things.

Being grateful and thankful for even the little, will suffocate complaining. Today, look for new opportunities where you can express your gratitude. Keeping your heart full of thanksgiving will grow your love!

The things I am thankful for about my husband are

_____

_____

I choose to be grateful instead of complaining!

Your gratitude is a supernatural door opener!

GRATITUDE IS A *door opener* FOR THE INCREASE *of my* BLESSINGS

Inhale God's presence today as you feel him hovering over you. He has all the answers you need!

Use these lines to record God's faithfulness.

_____
_____
_____
_____
_____
_____
_____
_____
_____
_____
_____
_____
_____
_____
_____
_____
_____
_____
_____
_____

Be kind and compassionate to one another, forgiving each other, just as in Christ God forgave you.
Ephesians 4:32

Tender moments to grow your love

Let Go

Do not hang on to offenses. Live every day with the tool of forgiveness. You will find yourself carrying offenses from days into weeks into months and into the next year without the grace of forgiveness. Do not expect perfection from your husband, just love and let grace grow within your heart! **Heaven is cheering you on!**

Connie had been married before, and she learned the importance of forgiving and letting go. After she had gotten divorced, she could not even remember why they had started fighting.

She met Carl; they fell in love and got married 6 months later. Her love for her husband Carl grew with her ability to forgive and let go. She experienced the importance of utilizing the tool of forgiveness. No matter what happened or what was going on, Connie chose to forgive Carl. She refused to go to bed upset.

Do you think Connie's actions of forgiving and letting go had am impact on her marriage? She practiced letting go of offenses, the second it happened! Her ability to forgive and let go, had an enormous impact on Carl.

You will find forgiveness a needed tool for the success of your marriage and any relationship. As you practice forgiving your husband and others in your life, you will find forgiveness growing within your heart! Letting go of offenses will always grow your love! Remember what you feed will grow. As you feed your love, you will find it growing rapidly!

I choose to let go of

_____
_____
_____
_____

I choose to bless those who have hurt me!

Forgiveness keeps you free!

I BREAK THE CHAINS OF UNFORGIVENESS FROM YOU AND FREEDOM IS YOURS

As you spend time with God today, write down the things he shares with you as he shows you how to love your husband.

Use these lines to record God's faithfulness.

_____
_____
_____
_____
_____
_____
_____
_____
_____
_____
_____
_____
_____
_____
_____
_____
_____
_____
_____

Finally, brothers, whatever is true, whatever is noble, whatever is right, whatever is pure, whatever is lovely, whatever is admirable, if anything is excellent or praiseworthy, think about such things. Philippians 4:8

Tender moments to grow your love

Stay Humble

When you disappoint your husband or let him down, be quick to apologize. Your ability to be quick and ready to apologize will grow your love! God loves your humility and as you continue to plant seeds of goodness, you will reap a harvest of benevolence.

Olivia was bright, beautiful, and full of high-energy. She was in love with Oliver. The two of them got married and synchronized their schedules so they could spend more time together. Olivia's car broke down and she needed to borrow Oliver's vehicle. He did not mind Olivia borrowing his car. He just asked her to keep it clean and to wash it before she parked it in the garage.

Olivia had a work meeting to attend and when she got home, she parked it in the garage. Unfortunately, she forgot to wash his vehicle and she left a bag in the front seat. When Oliver noticed her back so soon, he asked her, "Did you wash the car?" She looked at him and said, "Oh baby, I am so sorry, I forgot!" She reached for his keys and said, I will go wash it now. Oliver smiled, and said, "My love that is okay, don't worry about it, I can wash it tomorrow." The two of them sat down that night, enjoying a movie and a midnight snack. They laughed together and talked about their plans for the coming year!

Do you think Olivia's quickness to apologize set the mood in their house for grace and love? Today search your heart for anything you may need to make right with your husband. Saying, "I am sorry," when you have offended him will increase your marital honor and respect! Practice your humility on the lines below and grow your love into a better place!

My love, I am sorry for

_____
_____
_____
_____
_____

My husband is a gift from God I honor and value!

> *Loving your husband enough to admit when you are wrong is totally stunning!*

FOR I LONG

to show you more,

I LONG TO GIVE YOU MORE,

come closer into my presence

God hovers over you with answers to the questions that lay upon your heart.

Use these lines to record God's faithfulness.

A hot-tempered man stirs up dissension, but a patient man calms a quarrel. Proverbs 15:18

Tender moments to grow your love

Don't Be a Right Fighter

Guard against being a right fighter. Remember you are on the same team. Focus on working together, more than who is right. You will find your love growing as you nurture your ability to be a team. God enjoys your teamwork.

William and Mable had been married 2 years. They loved each other but were struggling with some issues between them. William had a habit of always thinking he was right, even when he was wrong. Mable did not help matters with her inability to discuss their issues. One day Mable decided she needed things to change. She spent time with God and asked Him to help her be the loving wife William needed. She already knew God had seen all the wrong and instead of pointing her finger at her husband, she opened her heart and asked God to help her be a better wife. As Mable spent time in God's presence, she felt him filling her heart with his love and peace.

When she was done praying, she went to find her husband. William was outside, sitting on the swing. She walked over to sit beside him and asked him if he would forgive her. "For what," William said. her loving response caught him off guard. She looked at him and told him she had prayed to God asking Him to help her be a better wife. William looked back at her, and said, "My love, I need to be a better husband." The two held hands as they exchanged apologies to each other for even the little things. Their apologies soon turned into laughter as they both found it funny as each of them began to express their feelings about the small stuff.

William had an extensive list of things he asked his loving wife to forgive him for and as Mable listened to him, she could not keep the tears from running down her face. She loved this man more than she knew, and she found the love of God flooding both of their hearts.

William asked Mable if she would go to church with him on Sunday and she agreed. The two joined hands together and prayed, asking God to help them love each other better. They began to grow their love as they put the feelings of each other above their own. Their love removed any need to be a right fighter and William realized he did not need to be right to be loved by Mable.

Do you think Mable's prayer to God helped her be loving and kind to her husband? As a wife, you will find your time with God to be priceless as he fills your heart with his love, you can then share that love with your husband! Today take time to search areas in your heart where you have been a right fighter. Remember you and your husband are on the same team. God enjoys your love and unity!

> *Thinking about your husband above yourself is gold!*

To refrain from being a right fighter, I will ...

_____
_____
_____
_____
_____
_____
_____
_____
_____
_____
_____
_____
_____

My husband is a gift from God, and I know we are a team!

AND I WILL

Increase

YOUR
HOPE AND GIVE
YOU PEACE

As you spend time with God today, write down the things he shares with you as he shows you how to love your husband.

Use these lines to record God's faithfulness.

_____
_____
_____
_____
_____
_____
_____
_____
_____
_____
_____
_____
_____
_____
_____
_____
_____
_____
_____
_____

Give, and it will be given unto you. A good measure, pressed down, shaken together and running over, will be poured into your lap. For with the measure you use, it will be measured to you. Luke 6:38

Tender moments to grow your love

Be A Giver

Cultivate a heart of giving. When you live with the attribute to give, it will have a significant impact on your marriage and life. Giving will suffocate selfishness. Give your time, heart, tithe, and love to God first, then your husband!

Elijah and Isabella met at church and were faithful in their time and service to God along with their tithe. There was nothing Isabella would not do for Elijah. She had started her own business which was flourishing. Elijah worked for a major corporation as a lawyer and the two enjoyed their evenings together in the small town of Clearwater. Elijah came home one day, concerned about his job. His corporate boss was asking him to relocate to Deshler. Elijah did not know how Isabella was going to take the news.

She was always willing to relocate, but selling her business was a big ordeal!

Isabella got home that day and noticed Elijah bothered by something. She asked him, "What is wrong?" Elijah answered her by saying, "His boss wanted to relocate him to Deshler." Isabella laughed and said, "Is that the only thing bothering you?" She looked at Elijah and said, "Then we relocate, sell the business and buy a new place there." We have done it before, and we can do it again. "Don't worry about the small stuff my love," she said as she noticed the worry filling Elijah's eyes.

He smiled and his face relaxed. He was truly blessed to have such a giving wife. He looked at her and said, "I am blessed to have you for a wife." Isabella said, "No my love, we are blessed to have each other!" Their love grew as they continued to give to each other unconditionally.

Do you think Isabella's ability to think about her husband above herself, nurtured their marriage? As a wife you will receive multiple opportunities to be a giver and think first about your husband or focus on your own needs alone.

Today think about areas in your life where you can give in a greater measure. Your giving will grow your love and affect every area of your life!

I enjoy giving

_____
_____
_____
_____
_____
_____
_____
_____

I can give in greater measures to my husband by

_____
_____

_____
_____
_____
_____
_____
_____
_____

My giving will grow my love!

> *Your ability to give will grow your marital love immensely!*

your
GIVING REFLECTS
the goodness
OF MY HEART

Inhale God's presence today as you feel him hovering over you. He has all the answers you need!

Use these lines to record God's faithfulness.

Each of you should look not only to your own interests, but also to the interests of others. Philippians 2:4

Tender moments to grow your love

Make a Full Investment

Invest fully in your marriage. Put your heart and soul into your relationship and love your husband fully. He will know when you are emotionally connected. Love him enough to give him your thoughts, ideas, concerns, and your loving emotions. Viewing your husband as your best friend will grow your love immensely!

Ava knew Lucas before they got married. Lucas worked with Ava, and he knew she was a dedicated woman to her work and him. After long conversations together, she decided to quit her job so she could care for their newborn twins, Allen, and Alex. The boys had grown fast and were now in first grade. Ava decided to go back to work so Lucas could work on his music. This young couple were completely invested in their marriage and each other. There was nothing either of them would not do for the other. They grew their love as they invested fully in their marriage and life together.

Do you think Ava's commitment to her husband and their family helped nurture their relationship? As a wife, you will find yourself blessed with many opportunities where you can grow your marital investment. This superb wife utilized these opportunities to gain experience and grow her commitment.

Today take time to think about the many ways you can increase your marital investment. Remember your total investment will grow your love and nurture your husband's heart! God enjoys your full commitment to each other!

To increase my marital investment, I will

_____

_____

_____

_____
_____
_____
_____
_____
_____
_____
_____
_____
_____
_____

Marriage is a gift from God and my full investment into my marriage will grow our love!

> Your commitment to God will help grow your commitment to your husband!

YOU WILL STAND AND CALL ME MIGHTY IN YOUR MIDST

God hovers over you with answers to the questions that lay upon your heart.

Use these lines to record God's faithfulness.

_____
_____
_____
_____
_____
_____
_____
_____
_____
_____
_____
_____
_____
_____
_____
_____
_____
_____
_____

Each of you should look not only to your own interests, but also to the interests of others. Philippians 2:4

Tender moments to grow your love

Consider the Timing

Timing is everything. Even though you may be upset or bothered by something, it might not be the right place or time to discuss it. Be wise and show your consideration by waiting for the right time to discuss your concerns. Keep nurturing your love.

Sophia enjoyed picking Mason up from work. She loved the conversations they had, as they chatted driving home. Mason would tell her about his day with all the unexpected details. He would always ask Sophia about her day, wanting to know how her day had gone.

It was Tuesday, and Sophia had gotten a letter in the mail she did not understand. She picked up Mason as she always did, but today, he was different. He was not his bubbly self. Sophia decided not to mention the letter until she knew he was okay.

That night at the supper table, Mason apologized for being quiet and told Sophia, he had just gotten laid off. Sophia got up from the table and went over to give Mason a hug. "Honey," she said, "Don't worry, everything will be fine." Mason relaxed, as he heard the soothing words of his wife. The two went to bed and Sophia decided to discuss the letter at breakfast. This wise couple grew their love, as they put the feelings of each other, above their own.

Do you think Sophia's ability to consider the timing, helped nurture their relationship? As a wife, you will find your timing to discuss sensitive matters, very crucial! Your consideration in verbalizing even the delicate things will grow your love immensely!   Sophia mastered the capacity to consider the timing of her concerns she needed to discuss. Today, take time to think about the timing of your affairs.

You will find yourself wise as you consider the feelings of your husband. Keep growing your love!

To consider the timing of my concerns, I will,

_____
_____
_____
_____
_____
_____
_____
_____
_____
_____
_____
_____
_____
_____
_____

_____
_____
_____
_____
_____

My husband is a priceless gift from God, and I will consider the timing of my concerns to honor him!

> Utilizing the technique of timing is an amazing love skill!

I DELIGHT IN
your love and unity
AND I WILL INCREASE WHAT
you have to a greater measure

Inhale God's presence today as you feel him hovering over you. He has all the answers you need!

Use these lines to record God's faithfulness.

_____
_____
_____
_____
_____
_____
_____
_____
_____
_____
_____
_____
_____
_____
_____
_____
_____
_____
_____
_____
_____

My commandment is this: Love each other as I have loved you. John 15:12

Tender moments to grow your love

Compromise

Now that you are married, think about your husband. Remember the world does not revolve around you. Work on being flexible and embracing compromise even when you want your own way. Your flexibility is a needed tool for the success of your marriage.

Ethan and Mia had not dated long before they fell in love and decided to get married. They worked the same schedule and enjoyed spending time together. Mia recalls their first month together as a bump in the road. She remembers needing to compromise when they went out to eat. Mia quickly learned new foods, she thought she hated, but really loved! Ethan learned to compromise as well and recalls learning to love foods and sports he thought he did not like. These two were married and best friends.

They enjoyed the experience of learning new hobbies, foods, and activities together. This young couple became wise with life as they valued each other enough to compromise when they needed to.

Do you think Mia's willingness to compromise helped nurture their relationship and grow their love? As a wife you will find yourself faced with occasions where you can implement the tool of compromise. Today take time to think about the many ways you can put your husband first. You do not have to like the same foods, hobbies, or interests. Learning to compromise and give in your relationship will go a long way!

I can compromise in a greater way by,

_____

_____

I will think more about my husband's feelings when we,

_____

_____

_____

_____

_____

_____

My husband is a gift from God I will value and treasure!

Thinking about my spouse is fun!

I AM *your* LASTING *hope*

As you spend time with God today, write down the things he shares with you as he shows you how to love your husband.

Use these lines to record God's faithfulness.

_____
_____
_____
_____
_____
_____
_____
_____
_____
_____
_____
_____
_____
_____
_____
_____
_____
_____

So, I recommend the enjoyment of life, because nothing is better for a man under the sun than to eat and drink and be glad. Then joy will accompany him in his work all the days of the life God has given him under the sun.
Ecclesiastes 8:15

Tender moments to grow your love

Find the Fun

Focus on making your marriage an adventure. Be spontaneous, adventurous, plan at times and always engage in your love life together with gratitude for each other. Embrace the unexpected with fun, creating memories for tomorrow. Planning is great, but spontaneous moves can bring adventure and fun into your marriage. Take time to think about ways you can plan at times but also be spontaneous.

Alex and Ella had been married 2 years. They were opposites and they loved the fun each of them brought into their relationship. Alex got up one morning before Ella. He packed a suitcase for them both, then he put their travel bags in the trunk of their car. When Ella got up,

Alex told her they were going on an adventure. "Where?" she asked. Alex looked at her and said, "Where would you like to go?" She laughed, not knowing he was really being serious. Alex drove her to the airport and told her to pick a location. She picked Florida, and off they went. They boarded a plane and landed with no place to go, but the adventure of the experience. Alex rented a car for the day and took Ella to a restaurant of her choice. They booked a return trip home the following day. As they boarded the plane, Ella looked at Alex and said, "Baby, thank-you for marrying me!" They both had experienced the fun in adventure.

    Do you think Ella's ability to be flexible helped nurture their relationship? She could have refused to go on the trip, feeling the need to plan. Instead, Ella adapted to the situation and went with the flow. As a wife you will receive multiple opportunities to relax and follow your husband even when you do not have everything planned out. Your trust in allowing your husband to lead will grow your love by leaps and bounds.

Today look for ways you can embrace spontaneous adventure in your marriage. If your husband plans a trip, just go with the flow. Learn to plan at times, with the ability to be spontaneous and adventurous. The experience will bring the fun of love into your marriage!

Your love skills are growing!

I can increase spontaneous fun in our marriage by,

_____
_____
_____
_____
_____
_____
_____
_____
_____

_____
_____
_____
_____
_____
_____

I embrace ways I can bring spontaneous adventure into our marriage!

> *Relax, and enjoy your marital journey!*

you will
REST IN THE
goodness of my
LOVE

God hovers over you with answers to the questions that lay upon your heart.

Use these lines to record God's faithfulness.

_____
_____
_____
_____
_____
_____
_____
_____
_____
_____
_____
_____
_____
_____
_____
_____
_____
_____
_____
_____
_____
_____

Do everything in love. I Corinthians 16:14

Tender moments to grow your love

Learn to Engage

When your husband discusses things, you have no interest in, focus on engaging him. Listening to him will allow you to deepen your understanding of him. This will grow your love and nurture your marriage. Your love skills are growing!

Brendon and Becky had been married 6 months. Brendon was a chemist and Becky worked as a manager at the local convenient store. They both worked the same hours and relished their date nights together. Brendon always enjoyed telling Becky about his day and the events that had taken place. Becky listened attentively to Brendon even when she was tired and feeling sleepy. She found her understanding of her husband growing the more she listened to him talk. When Brendon was done communicating, he always asked Becky about her day, and she loved giving him the details of her workday with the new events that had happened. This young couple grew their love into a deeper place as they listened to the hearts of each other!

    Do you think Becky's ability to listen to her husband about even the smallest details that did not interest her, helped grow their love? She learned many new things about him as she listened to the heart of her husband. Today think about the many ways you can engage with your husband in a greater way. Engaging with your spouse on matters you have no interest in will make you wise!

To engage with my husband in a greater way, I will...

_____

_____

_____
_____
_____
_____
_____
_____
_____
_____
_____
_____
_____
_____
_____
_____

Engaging with my husband, will grow our love!

> *Your marital participation will grow your love extraordinarily!*

YOU ARE A *carrier of life* AND *you transform* ENVIRONMENTS WITH MY LOVE

Inhale God's presence today as you feel him hovering over you. He has all the answers you need!

Use these lines to record God's faithfulness.

_____
_____
_____
_____
_____
_____
_____
_____
_____
_____
_____
_____
_____
_____
_____
_____
_____
_____

Again, I tell you that if two of you on earth agree about anything you ask for, it will be done for you by my Father in heaven. Matthew 18:19

Tender moments to grow your love

Pray Together

Pray together daily. If you are not feeling the unity, put everything aside and engage in a harmonious prayer. Your hearts touching God will always be a healing regimen. Take time to think about the many ways you may need God to move on your behalf. It could be financial, work, health, etc. Make a list of these needs and pray about them together with your husband! God will hear those things you speak. He will move mountains as you experience miracles!

Your love will be strengthened, as you pray together daily with God.

Martin and Mandy had just gotten married. They became smitten with each other the day they met. This couple dated each other and said their, "I do's," to seal the deal. They both had been raised in a Christian home and they knew the importance of praying together. No matter what happened, they knew they could trust God with anything!

    Three weeks after they were married, Martin was in an automobile accident. He broke his vertebrae and found himself unable to walk. Mandy prayed with her family and Martin believing God for a miracle. The doctors told them they did not think he would be able to walk again, but only time could tell. Mandy would not allow her heart to absorb what the doctors had said. She stood believing God for a miracle. Three months later, Martin woke up with feeling in his legs. Martin and Mandy cried together as they thanked God for their miracle. Martin began therapy and 1 month later, he was walking with a cane. Mandy and Martin had learned the importance and benefits of praying together. This couple became wise with their time together with God.

Do you think Mandy's resource to pray and trust God, had an impact on their marriage? As a wife, you will find the strength of your relationship with God pulling you through even the hardest times. Standing strong and believing God for even the impossible will be priceless. Today take a moment to think about a time daily when you can pray for your husband. Taking your requests to God will grow your faith and love!

I will pray daily for my husband at

_____o'clock.

My prayers will grow our marital love!

> Your marital prayers will move mountains!

YOUR *unity* IN PRAYER *moves my* HEART

As you spend time with God today, write down the things he shares with you as he shows you how to love your husband.

Use these lines to record God's faithfulness.

_____
_____
_____
_____
_____
_____
_____
_____
_____
_____
_____
_____
_____
_____
_____
_____
_____
_____
_____
_____

Therefore encourage one another and build each other up, just as in fact you are doing.   I Thessalonians 5:11

Tender moments to grow your love

Cultivate His Gifts

Look for the gifts and abilities in your husband's hand and help cultivate these gifts. Encourage him to be everything that God has purposed for him on earth. Thinking about the gifts in your husband's hand will make you wise. You can be the voice of encouragement, motivating him to be all that God has called him to be. **Heaven is cheering you on, while you stand as, his biggest cheerleader!**

Daniel and Evelyn were both young, in love and energetic. Daniel worked a full-time job at the hospital and Evelyn had her own business she ran out of their house. Evelyn loved to paint, and Daniel enjoyed writing music. This young couple lived to encourage each other in their hobbies and fun activities. They both grew their love as they became the breath of God to encourage each other in their gifts and abilities.

Do you think Evelyn's ability to seize every opportunity to build her husband helped grow their love and nurture their relationship? You will find your building words to your husband, the very inspiration he needs. Even though words of affirmation may not be his love language, when you speak, you will find yourself feeding his spirit!

Today think about the gifts and abilities in your husband's hand. What is he good at and how can you encourage him? God enjoys the way you encourage your husband to use all the talents God has placed in him.

My husband's gifts are

_____
_____
_____
_____
_____
_____

I choose to encourage my husband to be all that God has placed within him!

> _I motivate and inspire my husband to be all that God has purposed for him to be!_

YOU
represent
ME
well.

God hovers over you with answers to the questions that lay upon your heart.

Use these lines to record God's faithfulness.

_____
_____
_____
_____
_____
_____
_____
_____
_____
_____
_____
_____
_____
_____
_____
_____

Come, let us sing for joy to the LORD, let us shout aloud to the Rock of our salvation. Psalm 95:1

Tender moments to grow your love

Worship God Together

Take time to sing together, it may be in the car, at home or relaxing on the sofa. Singing together will always put joy in your hearts and grow your love into a better place. God loves the way you worship together. He waits daily to hear your praise!

Max was a worship leader at church and Melinda sang in the church choir. This couple loved to worship God together at church and at home. When Max started singing at home, Melinda always joined him, singing her melody, and harmonizing with her husband. This couple grew to be a firehouse for God. They felt blessed to be able to sing together at church, in their car and at home.

Do you think Melinda's attribute to sing with her husband helped grow their love? As a wife, your unity in even singing with your husband will grow your love. It is even the simplest things you may think to be insignificant that will nurture the unity and love between you both.

Today think about how you and your husband can incorporate a time for fun with singing worship songs together to God. Remember you do not have to sing well to lift praise to God. He enjoys all the melodies you lift to Him!

Our favorite songs are...

_____

_____

_____

_____

_____

_____
_____
_____
_____
_____
_____

Singing puts joy in our hearts!

> Your marital joy blesses those around you!

I HAVE PUT A SONG IN
your heart
AND THANKSGIVING
upon
YOUR LIPS

Inhale God's presence today as you feel him hovering over you. He has all the answers you need!

Use these lines to record God's faithfulness.

And my God will meet all your needs according to His glorious riches in Christ Jesus. Philippians 4:19

Tender moments to grow your love

Money Matters

Keep your love hats on when discussing money and do not sweat the small stuff. Work together as a team when budgeting and paying bills. Remember to make this a team effort. Acting like you have all the money answers can stifle your love. Learn from each other, grow your love, and reinvest your dividends.

Remember when you value your marriage; you will value your money. Investing in your financial future is an amazing way to grow your love!

Doug and Donna had been married 6 months, when they bought their first house. They had been saving even before they got married. This wise couple saved enough money to buy the house they were both looking at.

Doug was a financial advisor and Donna worked at the MidAmerican bank. They both had a mind for money, and they loved investing their money so they could watch it grow. This incredible couple went to church together and paid their tithe weekly. If you were to ask them today, how to grow their love, they would tell you to grow your money.

Do you think Donna's ability to respect the money they worked hard for, helped grow their love? As a wife, you will have multiple opportunities to engage with your husband on money matters or do as you wish. Seizing every occasion that comes your way to work together, with your husband, will make you wise.

Today, take the time to think about the many ways you can collaborate with your husband to invest financially for your future! When you value your marriage, you will value your money. Keep growing your love as you fill out the following lines!

I will collaborate with my husband on money matters by...

_____
_____
_____
_____
_____
_____
_____
_____
_____

We value our marriage by financially investing in our future!

> *Growing your money with your love is totally*

YOU WILL

Know

MY PROVISION AND
RECOGNIZE ME AS
YOUR PROVIDER

As you spend time with God today, write down the things he shares with you as he shows you how to love your husband.

Use these lines to record God's faithfulness.

Do nothing out of selfish ambition or vain conceit, but in humility consider others better than yourselves.
Philippians 2:3

Tender moments to grow your love

You're Differences

Embrace the differences in each other and accept your husband for who he is. Do not try to control or change him just enjoy his strength in the differences he portrays in your marriage. Remember you do not have to think alike, or even agree on the same things. Just agree to disagree and enjoy each other.

Adam and Abigail had gotten married despite all their differences. All the foods Adam loved; Abigail could not eat. Adam loved the cold sports, while Abigail was a freeze bunny. They always found fun in their differences and laughed through any trial. This young wise couple grew their love by embracing the differences of each other. They did not try to change each other but, merely accepted the opposites the other brought into their relationship.

Do you think ability to embrace their differences, help nurture their relationship? She was given multiple opportunities to complain about the contrast between them. Instead, she chose to embrace their distinctions and find the fun. As a wife, you will receive moments to complain or accept your husband's differences.

Today, look for the fun in your differences. Do not try to change your husband, just embrace his uniqueness. Finding the fun in your differences will be the spice your marriage needs! Stay fun and grow your love!

The opposites I embrace are

My husband likes,

_____
_____
_____
_____

I like,

_____
_____
_____

My husband's pet peeve is,

_____
_____
_____

My pet peeve is,

_____
_____
_____

We grow our love by embracing the differences in each other!

> *Celebrating your differences will make you wise!*

you are a carrier
OF HEAVEN'S DNA,
you leave goodness wherever
YOU GO

God hovers over you with answers to the questions that lay upon your heart.

Use these lines to record God's faithfulness.

_____
_____
_____
_____
_____
_____
_____
_____
_____
_____
_____
_____
_____
_____
_____
_____
_____
_____
_____
_____

The law of the LORD is perfect, reviving the soul. The statutes of the LORD are trustworthy, making wise the simple. Psalm 19:7

… Tender moments to grow your love

Do a Getaway

Be available for a getaway weekend. You will find the getaway will refresh your soul and recharge your love. Unplugging from the drum and everyday buzz around you will leave you both recharged.

Jack and Jeanette loved their getaway weekends. They would leave the last weekend of every month in June, July, and August. This amazing couple enjoyed the beach and the campground beside it. This couple would plan during the winter their getaways in the summer. Jack and Jeanette could not wish for summer to come any sooner! They lived for the warmth of the water and the refreshing beach. Jack would always feel recharged after a weekend at the resort. If Jeanette did not like the spot Jack had picked, she would focus on the bliss of being off work and away from the everyday buzz around them.

Do you think Jeanette's ability to flow with Jack when they were vacationing, helped grow their love? As a wife, it is important not to spoil your getaway time with complaining. Remember compromise is always needed and sometimes at the most unpleasant moments. Love well and choose to be grateful instead of complaining.

Today think about a resort, or getaway place you both can utilize to get recharged and refreshed. Think about the many places your husband would enjoy visiting on a getaway weekend. Make your list and when you plan your getaway, remember to think about your husband's desires, not just your own! Your love skills are amazing! Keep growing your love!

My husband would enjoy a getaway to,

_____
_____
_____
_____
_____
_____
_____
_____
_____
_____

When planning a getaway, I will consider my husband's like's first!

> *Enjoy and value your time together!*

I WILL *refresh* YOU IN MY *presence*

Inhale God's presence today as you feel him hovering over you. He has all the answers you need!

Use these lines to record God's faithfulness.

_____
_____
_____
_____
_____
_____
_____
_____
_____
_____
_____
_____
_____
_____
_____
_____
_____
_____
_____
_____

Be joyful in hope, patient in affliction, faithful in prayer.
Romans 12:12

Tender moments to grow your love

You're Actions

Your actions will always speak louder than your words so be careful of the things you do. You can caress the heart of your husband and grow your love with your actions. Keeping your responses and actions full of love is key! This is a priceless tool to practice daily. When you love with your gestures, your husband will be able to receive your words when you speak goodness to him.

Starla always had a way of showing her husband Steven, love actions with her words. She knew the importance of speaking good things, but she also knew it was just as important to show her love. Starla did both quite well. Steven had been in the military, and he had no tolerance for not being or doing what you say!

When Starla said she loved him she always proved it with her actions. Steven was always grateful to his wife for being a woman of her word. He appreciated the way her actions lined up with the things she said. Steven expressed his gratitude to Starla for her consistent love responses.

Do you think Starla's capacity to align her actions with her words, helped grow their love and nurture their relationship? Today take the time to think about all the loving ways you can tell your husband you love him! Remember to be intentional with your actions. Your words will never be louder than your actions! On the following lines record the many ways you can love your husband through your actions!

My love actions toward my husband are

_____
_____
_____
_____
_____

___

___

___

I can improve my love actions by

___

___

___

___

___

___

___

___

God loves the way I intentionally love my husband!

> *Your actions will speak louder than your words! wisely!*

you will hear love
THROUGH MY HEART
your response
WILL
be transforming

As you spend time with God today, write down the things he shares with you as he tells you how to love your husband.

Use these lines to record God's faithfulness.

_____
_____
_____
_____
_____
_____
_____
_____
_____
_____
_____
_____
_____
_____
_____
_____
_____
_____
_____

Marriage should be honored by all, and the marriage bed kept pure, for God will judge the adulterer and all the sexually immoral. Hebrews 13:4

Tender moments to grow your love

Stay Committed

Keep your eyes and admiration for your husband only. Remember to view him as a precious, priceless gift from God. Value commitment, as you esteem your husband with the highest regard. Your commitment to God will increase your commitment to your husband. **Heaven rejoices over your purity.**

Nancy loved Nathan. The day she said I do, became the best day of her life. She lived to love her husband and to give him her best. She had dated men before, but no one had loved her like Nathan. She was committed in her heart, soul, and actions. Her friends were not married, and Nancy chose not to hang with them, like she used to. They would look for cute guys on the internet and ask Nancy what she thought. When she told them, she was not interested they would laugh and make fun of her. She did not think they had taken her marriage seriously. She was married and committed. She wished her friends could respect her enough to accept that. Since they did not, she chose not to hang with them as often.

Nathan knew Nancy loved him and he was just as committed to her as she was to him. He saw the commitment and sacrifices his wife had given him and it had a lasting impact on him. These two grew their love as they daily chose to put each other first. Their commitment to one another grew as they protected their marriage and relationship.

Do you think Nancy's dedication and commitment to her husband helped grow their love? Her commitment to her husband, and their marriage spoke volumes to Nathan and those around them. As a wife you will be blessed with many opportunities to nurture your marriage and strengthen your commitment. You will find growing your love to be inspirational and energizing. There is nothing more beautiful than commitment!

Today take the time to think about the many ways you are committed and how you can increase your commitment to your husband.

I can increase my commitment to my husband by,

_____
_____
_____
_____
_____
_____
_____
_____
_____
_____

God enjoys the way I value my commitment to my husband!

Commitment will be seen through your decisions!

I AM YOUR LOVING DEFENDER

God hovers over you with answers to the questions that lay upon your heart.

Use these lines to record God's faithfulness.

_____
_____
_____
_____
_____
_____
_____
_____
_____
_____
_____
_____
_____
_____
_____
_____
_____
_____
_____
_____
_____

Her husband has full confidence in her and lacks nothing of value. Proverbs 31:11

Tender moments to grow your love

Honor Your Husband

Look for opportunities to show your husband honor and respect. As you view him as precious and priceless, you will cultivate value in your relationship. He will feel honored, and your love will grow immensely. Remember your actions are seeds. Continue to plant good seeds daily.

William and Annette had been married for 7 years. They flowed well together. People they met who did not know them, often thought they were newlyweds by, the way they loved each other. William trusted Annette and verbally expressed his gratitude to her for honoring and loving him. He always knew no matter what happened she would have his back. This made him grateful to be her husband! This amazing couple nurtured their relationship and grew their love. If you were to ask them how they stayed strong in their marriage, they would say, "with honor and respect for each other."

Do you think Annette's capacity to honor her husband at every moment, no matter what they were doing helped nurture their relationship? William felt her admiration and he made every attempt to love her back with high esteem. As a wife you will receive opportunities daily to honor and respect your husband. Utilizing every opportunity to love your husband will make you wise beyond your years!

Today take time to think about the many ways you honor your husband and how you can increase your admiration for him. **Remember your husband does not always have to be right, but he does need to be honored!** As you continue to nurture your husband's heart with honor and respect, you will find your love growing by leaps and bounds! Fill out the lines below and keep growing your honor.

I honor my husband by

_____
_____
_____
_____
_____
_____

I can increase my honor for my husband by,

_____
_____
_____
_____
_____

My honor for God helps me increase my honor for my husband!

I ENJOY the beauty YOU radiate as YOU HONOR each other

Inhale God's presence today as you feel him hovering over you. He has all the answers you need!

Use these lines to record God's faithfulness.

He who walks with the wise grows wise, but a companion of fools suffers harm. Proverbs 13:20

Tender moments to grow your love

Cultivate Friendships

Cultivate friendships with other married couples. Being married and hanging with only single friends apart from your husband can deplete your love. Ask God to bring Godly married friends into your life.

Owen and Grace had only been married 3 months when they decided they needed to hang with other married couples. Grace did not answer the phone calls from her friends and Owen noticed her pulling away from them. Their friends were all single and Grace expressed the desire one night to find some Christian young couples they could get acquainted with.

Owen and Grace went to the local Baptist church two streets away from their house. They began to attend their marriage class on Wednesday nights. They met 3 couples who had recently been married and they decided to invite them over for supper. Their friendships grew with these young married adults.

This wise couple knew they needed to cultivate friendships with other married couples to grow their love. Grace shared with Owen some of the things she learned from the other wife's and Owen shared as well, some of the things he learned from the other men. This wise couple embraced the wisdom they received from the other couples.

Do you think Grace's desire and willingness to cultivate Godly relationships, improved their marital connection? As a wife you will receive multiple opportunities, to grow your love and nourish the bond and friendship you have with your husband. Your role as a wife is huge and your actions will have an inspirational impact on your husband. Keep loving the heart you married and continue to grow your love!

Today take time to think about the things

you can do to cultivate friendships that will last for a lifetime. If you notice characteristics in your friends that are not Godly, be a proper example for them when you are together. God loves your commitment to each other!

Your love skills are growing!

Our married friends are

_____
_____
_____
_____
_____
_____

The things we have learned from them are,

_____
_____
_____
_____

_____
_____
_____
_____
_____
_____
_____
_____

Our friends are a blessing from God!

> Be the best friend
> you can be!

I HAVE GIVEN *you* UNLIMITED *increase all* AROUND YOU

As you spend time with God today, write down the things he shares with you as he shows you how to love your husband.

Use these lines to record God's faithfulness.

_____
_____
_____
_____
_____
_____
_____
_____
_____
_____
_____
_____
_____
_____
_____
_____
_____
_____

Trust in the Lord with all your heart and lean not on your own understanding; and in all your ways acknowledge Him, and He will make your paths straight.
Proverbs 3:5-6

Tender moments to grow your love

Grow Your Trust

Focus on growing your trust in your husband along with your trust in God. Think good things about your husband. Give him positive regard and always trust. You will find your trust for your husband growing as you deepen your belief in God.

Allison had been married for 5 years. She had known Nick for 2 years before they got married. Although Allison loved Nick, she struggled with the ability to trust him. Allison found herself surrounded by relationships and marriages that were dysfunctional. She had no positive role models in her life, but she wanted a better relationship. Allison prayed one day and asked God to help her trust, Nick. She wanted to be a good wife. She just needed help with her lack of trust and love at times. Allison decided to go to church one Sunday, and she asked Nick if he would join her. He agreed and they both went to church together. That Sunday Pastor Jenkins spoke on marriage and the gift of love. Allison absorbed everything she heard that day. She was determined to allow the words she heard to make a difference in her life and her marriage.

On Wednesday, Allison went to a women's group at their local church. The ladies were talking about their role as a wife and the importance of praying for their husbands. Allison listened to everything these ladies had to share. She enjoyed this love culture where the women of the church would come together and talk positively about their husbands and pray for them. When Allison left that day, she was feeling energized and motivated to connect with God. She had a desire to be a better wife. This church and the people here, made a massive impact on her marriage.

Allison started praying to God daily asking Him to show her how to love and trust her husband. God was always faithful in laying things on her heart. He showed her that trust was internal and as she trusted him, she could learn to trust her husband.

Do you think Allison's desire to connect with God and be a better wife, helped cultivate a marriage of love? As a wife you will find yourself surrounded by opportunities to pray and invite God into your marriage and relationship. This amazing couple grew their trust and love for each other with God at the center of their relationship!

Today take time to think about the many ways you can grow your trust in God and in your husband. Do you really trust God? Ask Him today to help you trust your husband! Your Love skills are amazing!

Your trust will grow your love!

Father God,

I ask you to help me trust you more! I know as my trust in you increases, I will be able to trust my husband. I put my trust in you and ask for your help today! Give me the strength and courage I need, to be the Godly wife you have called me to be. Help me to be the example You long for me to be. I love you God!

Amen.

List any areas where, you have not trusted your husband. Make the choice to give these areas to God today!

_____
_____
_____
_____
_____
_____
_____
_____
_____
_____
_____
_____
_____
_____
_____

_____

_____

_____

_____

_____

_____

Remember you don't have to feel trust, to believe your husband. *Trust God first and He will help you grow your trust for your husband!*

YOUR *trust in* ME INCREASES *your* TRUST IN *your husband*

30 Day Recap

YOU ARE

The joy

OF MY HEART

You are a woman after
MY own heart
and I will write My precepts
upon your heart and you will walk
in MY ways
and MY righteousness will guide you
As you love your husband
with MY love
you will be an example to many
of MY goodness
and forever faithfulness.

you
ARE A
woman
WHO
represents
MY LOVE

www.ingramcontent.com/pod-product-compliance
Lightning Source LLC
Chambersburg PA
CBHW060823050426
42453CB00008B/567